# Everyday Self-Care
## Lifestyle Rituals

# Everyday Self-Care

## Lifestyle Rituals

find greater meaning, connection,
and joy in daily life

## CICO BOOKS
LONDON · NEW YORK

Published in 2022 by CICO Books

An imprint of Ryland Peters & Small Ltd

20–21 Jockey's Fields      341 E 116th St

London WC1R 4BW          New York, NY 10029

www.rylandpeters.com

10 9 8 7 6 5 4 3 2 1

Text © Noelle Renée Kovary, Brenda Knight, and Sarah Sutton 2022

Design and illustration © CICO Books 2022

For text and image credits, see page 142.

A CIP catalog record for this book is available from the Library of Congress
and the British Library.

ISBN: 978-1-80065-086-2

Printed in China

Commissioning editor: Kristine Pidkameny

Senior commissioning editor: Carmel Edmonds

Senior designer: Emily Breen

Art director: Sally Powell

Production manager: Gordana Simakovic

Publishing manager: Penny Craig

Publisher: Cindy Richards

MIX
Paper from
responsible sources
FSC® C106563

# contents

# introduction

If you find it hard to take care of yourself, this book will teach you how incorporating rituals into all areas of your daily life can keep your body and mind replenished with energy and happiness. Creating helpful routines that work for you is a key part of your self-care journey.

Explore ways to show yourself the love and tenderness that you show to others. Discover the benefits of intuitive eating, which means listening to what your body needs, and simple breathwork, and incorporate mindful movement into every day. Treat yourself with regular luxurious baths and homemade beauty products, drawing on the healing properties of essential oils and natural ingredients.

Nurture your soul, too, by creating and repeating your own mantras and affirmations, as well as harnessing the power of crystals, moon energy, and the simple but essential act of gratitude.

With this handy guide, you will improve your health and happiness, and be able to fill every day with joy.

chapter 1

# RITUAL and ROUTINE

# your self-care journey

To know how to treat yourself, you first need to be aware of what you are trying to achieve. Understanding the things that will bring you into and out of balance is the key here. Taking a step back and looking at your life as one big picture is a great exercise to help you see where you need to improve and where you are doing great.

Keeping track of how things are now for at least a three-day period is recommended at the beginning of any wellness journey. This allows you to pick apart each category of health and happiness: diet, lifestyle, and sleep. All these components play a part in your health. Even the environment around you and what you choose to expose yourself to has a huge impact on your health. For example, if you work in a toxic environment, with negative people and high-pressure energy, this will have an effect on your mind, body, and spirit. Once you understand your unique constitution, you can begin to acknowledge and notice what brings you out of balance and what makes you feel your best.

Here are the types of things you should include in your notes, in as much detail as possible:

• **Sleep:** Make a note of any dreams you have, how many times you wake up, the quality of your sleep, and how you feel when you wake up.

• **Food and meal schedules:** Include what you have eaten and when, and how you feel emotionally and physically after you have eaten.

• **Daily activities:** Log activities such as sports, working out, going out, drinking, smoking, and dancing, and add notes about how they make you feel.

• **Exercise:** Be specific and note what emotional and physical responses are triggered when you exercise.

- **Bowel movements (this is for your eyes only!):** Record how you feel. Make a note of what your stool looks like (stiff, fully formed, mucus in it, or loose, for example). Document this every time you go to the toilet throughout the day.

- **Thoughts and memorable emotions:** Write down anything that stands out to you, anything that made you feel out of balance or really good. Be time specific!

Once you have completed your assessment for three days, review what you have written. (You have the option to continue keeping track in a journal if you like the activity.) It will give you an inside look at how you truly feel, what's aggravating you, what is working, and where your imbalance may be. The more honest and specific you are, the more beneficial this practice will be to your journey.

do something
every day that
brings you closer
to your goals

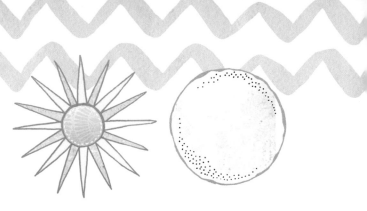

# creating routine

Having a strong daily routine can help you to balance your constitution, adapt your lifestyle to your unique mind-body nature, and promote self-care. To begin with, forming new routines can be challenging. Try writing out your routine and taping it to the refrigerator or a bathroom mirror so you can be reminded regularly of the things that will help you find balance.

If you forget to incorporate some of the tools on certain days, that's okay. These routines are designed to guide you toward a life full of wellness, not stress you out. Remember, this is a lifelong journey and these tools will always be available to you—this is not a temporary fix, this is a lifestyle shift.

The best routines are those that are customized to an individual's way of life and particular needs. Take the morning and evening routine suggestions on pages 16–45 and apply them to your own life in a mindful way.

# morning routine

The way we begin our day sets the tone for our energy, determining how we will feel throughout the day and how well we will sleep at the end of it. These are some of the best rituals to incorporate into your routine from when you wake up.

## rise with the sun

Going to sleep early and rising early keeps our bodies on a natural cycle that helps them function at 100 percent. It's best to wake up before 6 a.m., though in the winter, when the sun rises much later, it is okay to rise before 7 a.m. Unless you are a morning person, rising early may be a challenge for you. During the first couple of weeks, you may feel that switching your sleep schedule around is counterintuitive, but once you begin to rise early, you'll see all the ways your body and mind optimize energy throughout the day.

Give thanks and say an internal prayer upon waking up—every new day is a blessing. Make your bed when you wake up, too.

## meditate for at least five minutes

Early-morning meditation activates the bioelectric energy that helps to stimulate and direct energy to the pineal gland. The pineal gland is a pear-shaped gland in the brain that regulates hormone functions, specifically melatonin, which regulates our sleep-wake cycles. When we meditate in the morning, we are activating this system so that it can send more energy to our brains.

The act of meditation can help with focus, anxiety, mood disorders, energy levels, and overall mind-body balance. To meditate, sit in silence, focus on your breath, acknowledge any thoughts that come into your mind, and let them pass.

the better you
know your body,
the more you
can help yourself
feel better

## without force, eliminate

Our bodies accumulate a lot of toxins and waste while we sleep, which is why it's important to expel waste by emptying your bladder and bowels first thing in the morning. Regular elimination is an important function for our health. When we hold in or restrict the flow of elimination, it causes major stress on our bodies and organs.

If you are prone to constipation, a morning belly massage will aid in elimination. Use the tips of your index fingers to massage the small intestines in clockwise circular motions around the navel. Repeat a rotation of these circles three to five times. Do this massage while sitting on the toilet, preferably in a squatting position.

## wash your face

Wash your face with cool water and then gently wash your eyes with cool water as well. (Heat can build up in the eyes and cause irritation, so washing your eyes will help to keep them clear and calm.) Once you've washed your face, apply a refreshing toner to your skin, such as the Citrus-Rose Hydrosol (see page 100).

Washing your face and eyes with cool water upon waking up reduces inflammation and redness and invigorates the senses. This is honestly one of the simplest acts of kindness you can do for yourself in the morning (especially if you're not a morning person). It's not actually necessary to wash your face with skincare products in the morning unless you experience night sweats and feel that your skin is extra oily. You don't want to strip your skin of its natural oil.

# brush your teeth and scrape your tongue

Try incorporating the traditional Ayurvedic activity of tongue-scraping into your morning routine, after you've brushed your teeth. Scraping the tongue gets the body ready to digest and taste food. It also removes any toxins that have accumulated in the body overnight. It's important to remove these toxins as they may prevent the digestive system from functioning optimally. Once you add this activity to your morning routine, you won't want to go a day without it.

To scrape your tongue, hold a U-shaped stainless-steel or copper tongue scraper at both long ends, place the scraper toward the back of your tongue, taking care not to hit your teeth or go too far back to your tonsils. Using mild pressure, place the edge of the scraper on the back of your tongue and scrape toward the tip of your tongue in one fluid motion. Repeat this about five times, unless you feel that it hurts, which is a sign you have already removed all the excess toxins.

Always use a proper tongue-scraping tool; using something else, such as a spoon, could risk cutting the edge or middle of the tongue.

## Sip water with lemon juice

Drinking a mixture of warm water and fresh lemon juice in the morning will cleanse your bowels, promote digestion, and remove toxins.

Wash a lemon and then cut it in half. Squeeze the juice of one half into a large mug, then add the rest of the lemon to the mug. Heat 1½–3¾ cups (350–900 ml) water in a small saucepan on the stove until you see little bubbles forming at the bottom of the pan—do not let the water boil. Pour the warm water into the mug with the lemon juice.

Alternatively, if you don't have access to a stovetop, feel free to use a microwave. Heat the water in a microwave-safe cup (ceramic is preferred) in 30-second increments. Heating the water in a microwave for 40–50 seconds will usually warm the water to an enjoyable temperature.

If you are not used to drinking water first thing in the morning, start with just 1 cup (250 ml) of the water-lemon mixture, then build up to more when your body is used to it.

It's also good to consume warm water throughout the day—this aids detoxification, helps maintain a healthy weight, and keeps skin clear.

## get moving

Start your day with movement, such as yoga, Pilates, or cycling. Movement doesn't have to be intense—it can be as simple as stretching or walking. Movement helps keep circulation and blood flow healthy. Without movement, the body becomes stagnant. Moving first thing in the morning will wake up your body and give you more energy throughout the day.

## dry brush your body

Dry brushing your skin will kick-start your lymphatic system, which aids in detoxification. Dry brushing also keeps skin soft, removes dry or dead skin, and helps to maintain healthy circulation.

To dry brush your body, you will need a soft-bristle skin brush. Starting at your feet and using upward brush strokes, work your way up your body toward your heart. Dry brush your entire body, apart from your face. (See also pages 80–81.)

invigorate
your day

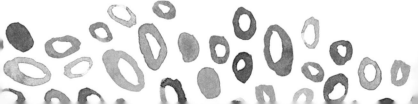

# infuse your shower or bath with essential oils

Most people don't have time to take a morning bath, but it's a beautiful way to start your day and set a positive energetic mood. Adding a couple of essential oils to your bathtub or shower in the morning will wake up your senses and invigorate your body. Citrus essential oils in particular aid in boosting mood and focus. See pages 82–89 for some healing bath recipes.

## invigorating essential oils

- **Lime** is a spirit lifter.

- **Jasmine** shifts moods upward.

- **Grapefruit** inculcates a feeling of happiness.

- **Peppermint** reduces stress and tension.

## massage your face

After washing, massage your face with a nourishing face oil, such as the Glowing Goddess Face Oil (see pages 98–99), to protect and hydrate your skin. Rub the oil into your hands and then apply generously to your entire face and décolletage area. Using upward strokes, pay particular attention to puffy areas by pressing and releasing along the inflamed regions. Very gently massage around the eye area as well, moving the soft tissue and skin in an upward motion and taking care not to get oil in your eyes.

# drink celery and lemon juice

Drinking a mixture of celery juice and lemon juice before eating food in the morning may help improve your overall health. Drinking celery juice on an empty stomach helps to produce hydrochloric acid, which breaks down proteins in the gut, restores electrolyte balance, detoxes the liver and kidneys, hydrates the skin, and lowers blood pressure. Celery also improves digestion, reduces inflammation, restores adrenals, reduces water retention, and lowers bad cholesterol levels. Additionally, celery is an excellent source of natural sodium, so it can help beat salty cravings when consumed daily.

Chop 1 bunch of celery and peel and halve 1 lemon. Add both to a juicer. Alternatively, if you don't have a juicer, put the celery and lemon in a food processor or blender and blend on a high speed until well mixed, then use a nut bag or cheesecloth (muslin) to strain the juice.

The juice mixture will keep for up to 2 days in an airtight container or jar in the refrigerator.

## enjoy your breakfast

It is important to eat breakfast before you start to work, teach, learn, or play. Food is our first form of medicine. Nourishing yourself with foods that are balancing to your body is important in the process of self-care. Without food, we have no fuel to burn.

Love not what
you are,
but what you
may become.

Miguel de Cervantes

# evening routine

So what's the secret to waking up happier and well-rested? It's a smarter nighttime routine and getting better sleep. Healthy physiological, psychological, and neurological functioning all depend on you getting enough quality sleep.

We all know that sleep is a basic human need, like eating and drinking, and yet many of us still believe that we can get by on less sleep with no negative consequences. In fact, obtaining a sufficient amount of quality sleep that's in sync with your body's natural internal clock is vital for your mental and physical health. Inadequate sleep is linked to a number of conditions, including heart disease, kidney disease, high blood pressure, diabetes, strokes, obesity, and depression.

What we choose to do with our evening hours directly impacts our quality of sleep, significantly influencing our mood and energy levels the next day. The truth is, most of us spend our nights binge-watching TV shows, texting, and late-night snacking—none of which are great for catching quality sleep. The good news: Revamping your bedtime

routine can be easy—and fun. The practices on the following pages will enhance your sleep, bring sacredness to your bedtime, and balance your body and mind.

## your sleeping sanctuary

Cultivating a soothing sleep routine will help you achieve the best sleep you'll ever have. As a starting point:

- Create a clean sleeping space.

- Invest in comfortable bedding.

- Keep the bedroom temperature low.

- Use nightlights if you have to get up for the bathroom during the night.

Organizing your bedroom to create an at-home sleeping sanctuary is key for keeping your mind relaxed and free of stimulation in the evening hours. Try to keep your use of electronic devices to a minimum and stop using them 30 minutes before bed.

## set the mood

Light candles and play sleep sounds to help you ease into bedtime. Take caution, however, and make sure to blow out candles before you fall asleep. Aromatherapy and diffusing essential oils also offer

a great way to create a sacred sleeping environment. Choosing a relaxing scent or blend to work naturally with your body will increase relaxation and promote restful sleep.

## relaxing essential oils

- **Roman chamomile** quells anxiety and soothes moods.

- **Frankincense** helps to calm breathing and nerves.

- **Geranium** is a natural sedative and releases negativity, stress, and depression.

- **Lavender** reduces tension, calms upset, and alleviates insomnia.

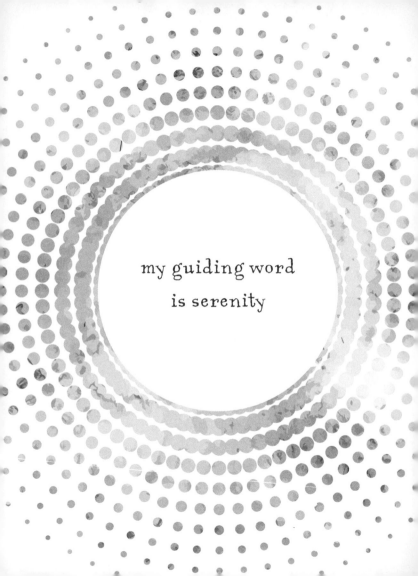

my guiding word

is serenity

# drink a warm spiced milk

Milk is the first thing we humans consume after birth. Drinking spiced milk is like nurturing yourself with maternal care before bed. The following recipe harnesses the healing properties of adaptogens (herbs, superfoods, and other substances that have nonspecific actions on the body, meaning they support all the major systems as well as regulatory functions).

Heat 1 teaspoon ghee in a saucepan over a low heat for 1 minute, then add ½ tablespoon ashwagandha powder, ½ tablespoon mucuna pruriens powder, and ½ teaspoon astragalus powder and simmer for 30 seconds. Add 1½ cups (350 ml) warm almond or other nut milk and stir. (If you have a hand-held milk frother or whisk, you may use it to froth the milk.) Remove from the heat. Once the liquid has cooled to a warm temperature, add 1 teaspoon raw honey.

Make drinking this adaptogenic milk an introduction to your evening routine, and sip it as you follow the next steps on pages 38–45.

## give yourself a massage

When warm oil is absorbed into the skin, it nourishes all parts of the body, enhances circulation, and stimulates the lymphatic system. The act of self-massage is a nurturing ritual involving the sense of touch. Oiling the external body helps to ground energy and relieve stress, which is helpful for winding down to sleep.

## give yourself a face mask

Paying attention to your head is a wonderful way to relax tight nerves and remove the stress of a long day. Make and apply one of the natural face masks from pages 93–97 and let the herbal infusion intoxicate and calm your senses.

# take a relaxing bath

Allowing yourself time to bathe in the healing power of water can be transformative. Taking a bath such as the Relaxing Chamomile Bath (see page 86) can be the perfect medicine for relaxing the body and mind after a hard day. The sensuous comfort water provides connects us back to both our bodies and the Earth's beauty.

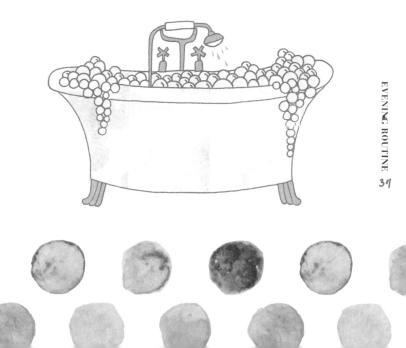

## write in your journal

Sometimes our minds take control of our senses and we can't rest because our mind isn't at rest. Journaling is a practice that can help soothe your thoughts and allow your mind to rest with ease. Keep a journal or notebook by your bedside and use it to write down your thoughts, whether it's a simple reminder, such as "don't forget to buy conditioner," a poem you're composing, or deep emotional feelings that need to be let out.

## prompts for journaling

The best part of my day was...

The hardest part of my day was...

The problem that's worrying me right now is...

The things I need to do tomorrow are...

Today I was thankful for...

Put your thoughts
to sleep. Do not let
them cast a shadow over
the moon of your heart.
Let go of thinking.

Rumi

# give yourself a reflexology foot massage

Reflexology involves stimulating the reflex points on your feet, hands, face, or ears to subtly impact the entire body, affecting the organs and glands. It can transport you into a state of deep relaxation where you are open to suggestions you give yourself. There are nearly 15,000 nerves in your feet alone, which is one of many reasons why foot reflexology is so calming, soothing, and effective. A simple foot-massage routine just before you go to bed can help you drift off to sleep naturally. Use an Ayurvedic massage oil such as Brahmi oil to help promote relaxation to the nerves and prevent insomnia.

To give yourself a foot massage, put 1 teaspoon of oil into the palm of your hand, rub your hands together and then massage the oil all over your feet. (If the skin of your feet is very dry, you may want to use more oil.) Using firm pressure, slowly massage along the arch of each foot. Massage back and forth along each foot, paying particular attention to any areas that feel sore. Do this massage for at least 10 minutes.

at close of day,
I find my place
of ease

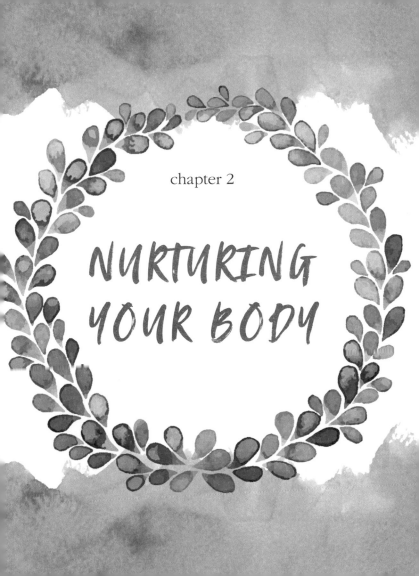

chapter 2

# NURTURING YOUR BODY

# intuitive eating

Intuitive eating is about having freedom around food. You can eat what you want, when you want without guilt, shame, sickness, bingeing, or triggering negative thought patterns. Practice intuitive eating by paying attention to how food makes you feel, how much food you want and need to eat, what food you actually enjoy, and what food affects your moods and physical body. The more you become acquainted with your body, the better you will feel. Your body wants to trust that you will fill it with balanced fuel; it actually gives you the ability to make the right decisions. Over time, it's common for our bodies to lose trust in our ability to nourish them. Letting go of the fear of who you truly are beneath the diets, labels, body image, and more will help you become happier and healthier in body, mind, and spirit.

you are in control
of this journey

## diet vs intuitive eating

When you give yourself permission to eat what your body wants and there are no "good" or "bad" foods, it acts like reverse psychology. Now that you can have whatever you want, you don't want it as much. Suddenly you can have one bite of something and be done with it, knowing that food is there for you if you want more.

Even though it's generally best to follow a lifestyle and nutritional plan that is going to balance your specific body, it's vital to know that you can still indulge in the food and drink you love the most.

## cravings

Learning to differentiate an emotional or memory craving from a
physical craving will help you eat intuitively. When the body needs
a nutrient, it sends signals to the brain so we eat those nutrients. In
a car, a little light comes on when it needs to be fueled or needs oil.
Unfortunately, we don't have it that easy and we must tune into our
bodies and question those signals to understand what we need. If you
ever notice yourself craving sugar, instead of letting that craving take
over, ask yourself the following questions:

- What did I eat today?

- Am I getting enough variety?

- Is my blood sugar low?

Your answers will help you discern what your body is truly
signaling you to eat.

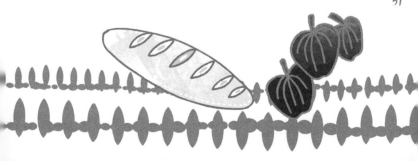

## beneficial cravings

There are such things as beneficial cravings and nonbeneficial cravings. Nonbeneficial cravings are usually linked to our emotional state. They can come up if we aren't nurturing our bodies and can cause feelings of tension, guilt, shame, or regret. If you eat a lot of junk food or skip meals often you may find yourself constantly craving oily, sugary, and processed foods. This can be an indication that you are stuck in a cycle of not feeding your body with nutrient-dense foods. Beneficial cravings mean that you are in control of what you are putting in your body and your emotions are not driving you to eat.

Our intuition is a great guide when it comes to making the best choices for ourselves. To implement this, start to notice what's going on in your body and mind when you crave a specific food. The more conscious and aware you are, the more you can nurture your body. When we trust our internal body cues over external diet rules we can begin to move and flow through life with more ease.

## refocusing common attitudes about food

| | |
|---|---|
| Can I have this? $\longrightarrow$ | Do I want this? |
| How do I look? $\longrightarrow$ | How do I feel? |
| How much food do I get today? $\longrightarrow$ | How much food do I need today? |
| Will this make me lose weight or gain weight? $\longrightarrow$ | Will this nourish me? |
| I exercise so I can eat. $\longrightarrow$ | I eat so I can exercise. |
| I can eat whatever I want on my cheat day. $\longrightarrow$ | I can eat whatever I want every day. |
| Food is my worst enemy and my favorite reward. $\longrightarrow$ | Food is just food. |

# conscious eating

Eating should be approached as a sacred and sensual experience. You are literally joining energies together. It's important to be mindful and conscious of your eating. Here is a simple yet effective ritual to increase your connection to your food.

## 1

Before you eat, feel and sense what your body needs and is truly craving. Make decisions about the food you are going to eat based on what is best for your body in that moment and what will serve you long term.

## 2

Once you have prepared your meal, sit in a calm and quiet environment, draw your attention to the food on your plate, and say a prayer, mantra, or blessing over your food. One of the main reasons why we say a blessing and infuse our food with positive energy is to help us remember that our food is energy. Food is fuel to nourish our bodies and it's important to honor that.

## 3

As you eat, slowly breathe in through your nose and out through your nose. Deep breathing will help you slow down and feel your food. Not only will you taste your food with heightened senses but also you will gain more energy from it.

## 4

Use the tools already embedded deep within your body. Chew your food as well as possible. The saliva in your mouth is loaded with digestive enzymes to help you break down your food before you even swallow it.

## 5

After you've eaten, draw attention to how each part of your body feels:

- Is the food giving you energy and love?

- Is your mind being nurtured?

- Do you feel you are absorbing all the nutrients?

- Do you feel happy?

Practice this ritual as often as you can. Choosing to be in a calm environment while you eat is choosing to heal your body through the practice of mindful eating. Try to abstain from negative conversation while you are dining with others—this will help your body stay in a calm and neutral state.

Happiness depends
upon ourselves.

Aristotle

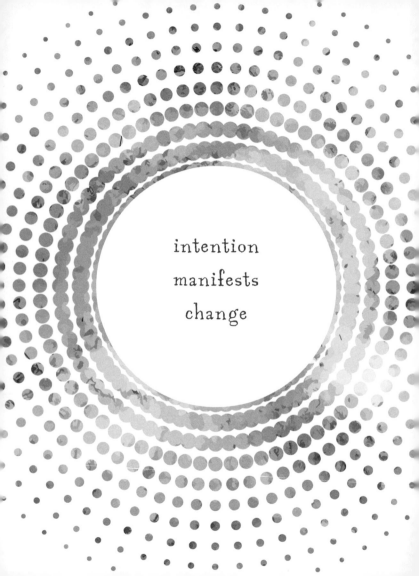

intention

manifests

change

# self-love and movement

It's difficult to stay active when you are busy taking care of kids, working long hours at a desk, spending time with family, or simply trying to do it all. However, movement is vital for your health (not just your physical health but also your mental health), so instead of looking at movement—whether it be yoga, the gym, sports, dance, or classes—as a chore, try thinking about moving your body as a form of self-love. The more we love ourselves, the more we thrive.

Every day you have an opportunity to honor your body by nourishing it, moving it, and loving it. When you stay active and keep your body in motion in an organic way that is a natural complement to the energetics of your body, you will find that life flows with more ease and less stress. Movement is a huge part of longevity and living a balanced life. When you move your body you are treating yourself with the respect you deserve. Your body deserves to be treated right 100 percent of the time.

You may find it difficult to stay motivated, but doing at least ten minutes of movement daily will really help your mind-body connection and create more space for healing. Movement can be done anywhere, at any time; every little bit you do counts!

# ways to stay active

• **Stretch, dance, jump around, and move as soon as you wake up in the morning:** Five minutes is all you need. This not only gets your energy up for the day but also wakes up all your body parts.

• **Walk or bike to work:** Doing some movement before you start work will increase your focus and prolong your energy. If your work is too far away to walk or bike, park your car farther away from your place of work and walk the longest distance possible to get there.

• **Stop, drop, and stretch:** Try to take a two-minute break from work every hour to move your body in an organic way. This will help you feel motivated and ready to work again. You don't only have to stretch, you could do push-ups, crunches, squats, planks, dance—whatever feels right to you.

• **Take a break:** Whether you work from home or elsewhere, you can add movement into your post-lunchtime routine. Light movement, like walking, is helpful for digestion after you have eaten. Either walk to a park to eat your lunch and then walk back, or take a walk around the block after you eat. If you live in a very cold climate and work in an office, just take a walk up and down the stairs if you don't want to go outdoors.

• **Do activities with friends:** It's much easier to stay motivated when you have a partner to help keep you accountable. Suggest going for a walk instead of meeting for tea to chat. Instead of going out to a bar, go to a salsa or Zumba class and shake your hips. There are plenty of fun activities you can do with others that will keep you connected while moving together.

## forest bathing

According to a recent EPA (Environmental Protection Agency) study, the average person spends 87 percent of his/her life indoors and 6 percent more in a car or commuting in buses or trains. We don't spend much time outside. Stress has a major impact on health and aging—spending time in nature is a way to counteract that and has been shown to reduce anxiety and increase relaxation.

Forest bathing, a practice begun in Japan in the 1980s, is growing in popularity and is blessedly easy. Forest bathers go to wooded areas and simply sit or stand in nature. Breathing in the air and taking in the earthy smells will bring your senses alive and, as a side benefit, regulate heart rate and blood pressure. Grab a camping blanket and set out to find a wooded area where you can be alone in the cathedral of nature. No phones! Find a spot, put down your blanket, and take off your shoes. Stand on the forest floor barefoot and feel the earth under your feet. You can either sit or lay down on your blanket for at least an hour and just be.

## eco walking meditation

Grounding is the technique for centering yourself within your being, getting into your body and out of your head. Grounding is how we reconnect and rebalance ourselves through the power of the element of Earth. This is the simplest of rituals, one you can do every day of your life. As you walk, take the time to see what is in your path. If it helps focus your mind, try taking a bag with you and picking up every piece of garbage in your path. Not only will it ground you, but it is an act of love for the Earth.

# prana: life-force energy

The Sanskrit word *prana* means both "life-force energy" and "breath"—it doesn't have a single direct translation or function. Prana is the root source of all the energy in the universe. All forces of nature are manifestations of prana. It is prana that keeps things moving in and around us. Without prana, life is gray, dark, cloudy, and full of stagnant energy. With prana, life is bright, creative, open, full, loving, and flowing. Prana can be found in the food we eat, the liquid we drink, the air we breathe, the warmth of the sun, and the people and places around us. This is why relationships feel so good—we are transferring this pranic energy from person to person.

Are you getting all of the prana you deserve? Answer the following questions as honestly as possible:

- Am I using my breath wisely?

- Am I gaining energy from the air I breathe, the food I eat, and the relationships I have?

- Do I utilize my full lung capacity?

- Am I aware of my surroundings?

- Do I gain strength from my breath?

- Do I deplete my energy with activities or people?

- Am I draining the energy of other people with my own energy?

- Is my life stressful and chaotic?

- Am I able to redirect negative energy into positive feelings?

- Is it hard for me to focus?

- Do I waste a lot of time and procrastinate daily?

- Are my thoughts, actions, and words overly self-critical and negative?

These questions are intended to help you see where you are on your journey, what areas you can improve upon, and where any imbalances may lie.

# breathe better

It seems pretty obvious to say that we need to breathe in order to live, but you can also use your breath to maximize your life span, combat stress, and manipulate the energetic flow (prana—see pages 64–65) in your body.

Think about your breath as a subtle force that not only fills your physical body with life-giving energetic oxygen but also fills your mind and emotional body with energetic vitality. When we inhale deeply and consciously, we breathe oxygen into our lungs as well as taking in the environment and knowledge found in all of life. What does it mean to be conscious of your breath? It means that you are aware of your own inhale/exhale and you can feel the energy of the air flowing in and out of your body.

inhale confidence,
exhale doubt

# deep breathing for clarity, calm, and focus

Your breathing is directly connected to your brain function and clarity of mind. Breath is controlled by your autonomic nervous system (ANS), which is affected by your thoughts. If you are feeling fearful or anxious, your thoughts will trigger the ANS to speed up your heart rate, raise blood pressure, and increase the speed and shallowness of your breath.

During every inhalation the heart rate increases slightly and during the exhale, the heart rate decreases slightly. This happens for everyone in every breath. As a result, you can wake up the body by taking a shorter inhale or de-stress by taking a longer exhale.

Take a breath in for a count of three. Slow the counts to one second by following each number with a word—for example:

1 mississippi, 2 mississippi, 3 mississippi

Then exhale for a count of six. You can also try inhaling for two and exhaling for four. As you lengthen your exhalation, instead of breathing out normally, try to hum as you do it. You might start off breathing shallowly but by the end of this practice you will be breathing diaphragmatically, from belly to nose. This is healing breath.

Deep breathing seems simple until you are experiencing stress and, without even knowing it, you'll begin breathing shallowly. Whenever that happens, try deep breathing as described above. Your stress will begin to fall away and your mental clarity will come into focus.

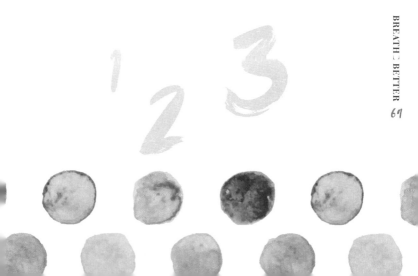

# restoring breath: murcha meditation

In Sanskrit *murcha* means "to retain," so this is the "retaining breath." Murcha will help you to hold on to some of the natural energy that work and life can drain away. This ritual is a yoga exercise for achieving a state of ecstasy through pranayama, or yogic breathing, which is the fine art of controlling the flow of oxygen in and out of the lungs. Conscious breathing can vastly improve your health and make you more alert. Done properly, murcha will enhance your mental capacity, center you, and create a sense of euphoria.

## 1

Sit down on the floor or a mat and make yourself as comfortable as possible. Now close your eyes and calm yourself completely. Begin the process of murcha by taking a few mindful breaths. Breathe through your nose. Don't hold your breath; just breathe in and out in a natural manner, but remain aware of your breathing.

## 2

When you are ready, take a deeper breath through your nose and visualize the new air and oxygen traveling throughout your body, cleansing and relaxing you. Hold that deeper breath, bend your neck,

and bring your chin as close to your lungs and chest as possible. Keep this position for as long as you can do so comfortably. When you need to, raise your head again and slowly exhale through your nose. When your lungs are empty, repeat the murcha breath.

### 3

Repeat this cycle of breathing five times only. After the fifth breath, notice how you feel and be "in the moment." Like most breathing meditations, you will experience a subtle sort of ecstasy with raised energy and a sense of bliss.

In pranayama, it is important to remember not to place any stress on your body. Don't hold your breath beyond your comfort level. To do so would be to go against the grain of the technique and teachings of pranayama.

With practice, you will notice you can hold your breath naturally and comfortably just a little bit longer each time. As with all things, pranayama gets better with practice.

# *increase prana and release stress*

This exercise is called a pranic breath. Start with one pranic breath and work your way up (in your own time) to ten. Do this practice at least once a day.

## *1*

Sit comfortably, cross-legged on the floor, if possible. You can use a bolster or blankets to prop your legs up or lean against a wall to help you sit up tall. Try to relax your shoulders, allowing your shoulder blades to roll down your back toward your waist. This will help to lift your chest up and create space for your ribcage to move freely.

## *2*

Place your palms together in front of your heart. Push with pressure against both palms to create an activation of energy within your body.

## *3*

Gently close your lips and focus only on breathing through your nose.

## 4

Inhale for the count of ten, breathing in deeply though your nose and drawing your breath down into your lungs. Feel the breath expanding in your ribcage and trickling down into your belly, expanding deeper and wider. Imagine this breath as a golden white light that is pulling in all of Mother Nature's beautiful invigorating energy and sucking it deep into your body.

## 5

Once your lungs and belly are full of this life-giving air, hold your breath for the count of ten (or as long as possible). Focus all of this energy to your third eye (the middle point in between your eyebrows). Imagine this space filling with all the golden white light that is building and swirling with prana.

## 6

Exhale for the count of ten. As you slowly exhale, imagine the golden white light showering over your whole body and leaving you energized and with all your senses vital.

The beginning is
always today.

Mary Shelley

chapter 3

# YOUR SANCTUARY SPA

# your bathroom

Turning your bathroom into a peaceful sanctuary is an easy way to slow down, bring love into your life, and treat your physical and emotional body with kindness.

A clean bathroom is just as important as a clean body. When we clean our bodies, we feel lighter, more balanced, and achieve a sense of clarity; the same goes for cleaning the spaces we live and function in. It is optimal to use all-natural, chemical-free cleaning supplies when setting the tone for your sacred space.

Aside from physically cleaning your space, you can take the process one step further and do a simple energy cleanse using either sage or Palo Santo smudge sticks (see opposite), which both cleanse stagnant energy and smell wonderful. Sage and Palo Santo have both been used for centuries to ward off negative people, emotions, situations, and energy. If you have lots of people coming in and out of your bathroom on a daily basis, cleansing the room is a good step to take so you can really heal in your sacred space and avoid picking up anyone else's energetic baggage.

## simple energy cleanse

### 1

Carefully light a sage or Palo Santo smudge stick, let it burn until you see smoke, and then blow the flame out.

### 2

Waft the smoke around the outline of your body (being careful not to touch yourself) and in the areas of your home where you wish to clear energy.

### 3

Once you've cleansed all the desired areas of your home, open a small window and let the negative energy out.

# divine detox: dry brushing

Your body rids itself of toxins via the lymphatic system. You can speed up that process by body brushing, gently stimulating the lymph nodes to do their job even more efficiently. Body brushes look like equestrian grooming tools and are easy to find at any bath and body store, health food store, or pharmacy. Always use a light touch when dry brushing and, afterward, apply a balm, such as In Your Groove Balm or Sweet Serenity Balm (see page 105).

You can double down on wellness by dry brushing before a bath as you are detoxing your skin and body, rehydrating your skin as you are soaking. One third of your body's toxins are excreted through the skin, the largest organ, and dry brushing helps to unclog pores and remove toxins that get trapped in the skin. A ritual that takes only five minutes a day offers so many health benefits, including the lovely bonus of a sense of deep serenity. All you need is a bathtub and a natural bristle brush with a long handle.

Remove your clothes and stand in the empty tub. Start brushing at the feet and move upward. Use long upward motions and brush all over your body, using a few brush strokes in every area. When done, rinse the tub thoroughly and rinse yourself. Scandinavians advocate rinsing in cold water too as that stimulates the blood to circulate, bringing more blood to the topmost layers of your skin

# healing bath recipes

Taking a bath is deeply therapeutic, providing benefits for both your mind and body. In ancient times, bathing was revered as a holy act of self-love.

## detox bath

These bath salts help to draw toxins out of the body and soften the skin, creating an invigorating experience.

**2 cups (450 g) Epsom salts**
**1 cup (225 g) baking soda (bicarbonate of soda)**
**10 drops of ginger essential oil**
**1 large lemon, washed and sliced**

*Makes enough for 1 use*

Fill your bathtub with warm water and then add all the ingredients. Soak in the bath for 20 minutes–1 hour.

## epsom salt

Salt is known for its ability to trap negative energy and clear it from a person, space, or object. Epsom salt is the most basic and potent salt you can add to your bath. Epsom salts reduce stress, eliminate toxins, and decrease pain, inflammation, and bloating.

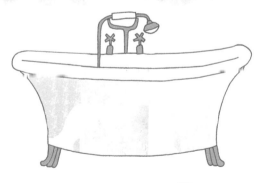

# rose milk bath

You couldn't dream up a more luxurious bath for your skin than this concoction. The lactic acid in the milk helps to remove dead skin, while the rose oil calms and tones new skin.

**1½ cups (190 g) milk powder (raw if available)**
**½ cup (130 g) Himalayan pink salt**
**1 handful dried or fresh rose petals**
**10 drops of rose essential oil**

*Makes enough for 1 use*

Put all the ingredients except the rose petals in a bowl of warm water and stir until the milk powder and salt dissolve. Fill your bathtub with water, then add the milk-and-salt mixture and sprinkle in the rose petals. Soak in the bath for 20 minutes–1 hour.

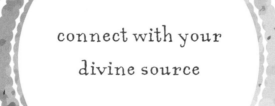

connect with your
divine source

# relaxing chamomile bath

Chamomile has a grounding effect, and the color and aroma of the flower petals, if using, will also help you reconnect your body to the Earth. The ashwagandha powder can help calm and relax nervousness and anxiety, while magnesium flakes are crucial for the remineralization of the body.

**1 cup (225 g) magnesium flakes**
**10 drops of chamomile essential oil**
**½ cup (70 g) ashwagandha powder**
**1 handful fresh rose petals, lavender, chamomile,
or other wildflowers (optional)**

*Makes enough for 1 use*

Put all the ingredients except the fresh flowers, if using, in a bowl of warm water and stir until the magnesium flakes and ashwagandha powder dissolve. Fill your bathtub with water, then add the bath salt mixture and sprinkle in the flowers, if using. Soak in the bath for 20 minutes–1 hour.

## if you don't have a bathtub

If you don't have a bathtub, you can use the recipes on pages 82–86 in a footbath. You can adjust the quantities of the ingredients to the amount of water you are using or make the footbath more potent by leaving the recipes as they are. Make sure the water in the footbath comes up to your ankles.

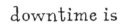

downtime is
your time

## baking-soda basics

Baking soda (bicarbonate of soda) is great in a bath and is very calming to the skin. Add a cup (130 g) under the faucet (tap) as you fill your tub with hot water.

If you suffer tension headaches, a simple solution is to treat it with a teaspoon of baking soda dissolved in a cup (225 ml) of warm water with ¼ cup (60 ml) of freshly squeezed lemon juice. Drink the mixture at room temperature and soon you'll feel fine.

# enhance your bath

Customize your bathing experience and create unique self-love rituals.

- **Sounds:** Set the mood with soothing tones. Listening to the sounds of nature and different vibrational frequencies can help you tap into the Earth element. Sounds can bring feelings of relaxation or levity, and they allow us to drop our menial thoughts and help us to focus inward.

- **Candles:** The sacred element of Fire can be introduced with candles. Use as many unscented candles as possible. Put a couple of candles on the inside corner of your bathtub or just leave them on a shelf in your bathroom. Whether you take a bath in the morning, at midday, or at night, using candles will surround you with natural light instead of stimulating or tiring your eyes with artificial light bulbs. This natural light will bring ease, calm, and a sense of sacredness into your space. Important: Never leave a burning candle unattended.

- **Essential oils, herbs, and flowers:** You can use essential oils to heal on an emotional and physical level. Dry herbs, flowers, fruits, and plants can all bring us the essence of Mother Earth and help us connect to a deeper healing, as well as infusing our bathwater with heightened energetics. For example, citrus fruits are uplifting and

roses evoke feelings of beauty and love. Take a dying bouquet of flowers from your home and, instead of throwing them in the trash, scatter the petals in your bathwater. For a cleansing and enlivening shower or bath, attach a bunch of eucalyptus leaves to the top of your shower head or under the bath tap before turning on the water.

- **Incense:** Incense provides a beautiful way to invoke the element of Air. It has been used for centuries in prayer and offerings to higher powers. By lighting incense after you cleanse your space, you are inviting positive radiant energy and spirit to fill your room.

# natural beauty recipes

Although beauty ultimately comes from the inside out, we can always do more to protect, heal, and prevent our skin from aging. At-home facials not only keep your skin looking radiant, but also make your whole body feel relaxed and beautiful. Using natural ingredients in your beauty recipes makes the whole process of skincare more sensual.

If you like, you can do a face mask with a partner or friend to help you connect with them on a deeper, more soulful level. You could use different face masks as often as three or four times a week, but it's not necessary to do them more often than three times a month if you don't have the time.

# moringa mermaid mask

Moringa powder has antiseptic qualities. It fights and heals acne, reduces inflammation, is rich in vitamin A and amino acids that help produce collagen, and balances the skin's pH.

**3 tablespoons water**

**juice of ½ lemon**

**½ teaspoon pearl powder**

**2 tablespoons raw honey**

**1½ tablespoons moringa powder**

*Makes enough for 1–2 uses*

Cleanse and dry your skin. Mix all ingredients together in a small bowl until smooth. Apply the mask to your face with your fingertips or a facial-mask brush, lightly massaging it into your skin. Leave the mask on for 15–20 minutes. Rinse off the mask with warm water.

Any leftover mask will keep for up to 4 days in an airtight container in the refrigerator. When using the mask for the second time, you may need to add a little extra water to the mixture, one drop at a time, to loosen the mask to a useable consistency.

# sandalwood shakti mask

Nutmeg and sandalwood have been used in Ayurvedic medicine for centuries to treat rashes, inflamed skin, cystic acne, and blemishes. It's an ideal face mask for anyone who is prone to acne due to its antibacterial and cooling properties.

**1 tablespoon ground nutmeg**
**4 tablespoons whole milk (raw if available)**
**2 tablespoons sandalwood powder**
**1 tablespoon raw honey**

*Makes enough for 1–2 uses*

Cleanse and dry your skin. Mix all the ingredients together in a small bowl until smooth. Apply the mask to your face with your fingertips or a facial-mask brush, lightly massaging it into your skin. Leave the mask on for 15–20 minutes, lying down with a towel beneath your head so the mask doesn't drip on anything (this mask tends to be a little watery). You may feel a tingling or stinging sensation while the mask is on. That is okay, the mask is working. Rinse off the mask with cool water.

Any leftover mask will keep for up to 4 days in an airtight container in the refrigerator. When using the mask for the second time, you may need to add a little extra milk to the mixture, one drop at a time, to loosen the mask to a useable consistency.

# blossoming beauty mask

Use this exfoliating mask once or twice a week to brighten your complexion and tighten pores.

½ cup (100 g) goat milk yogurt (raw if available)

½ teaspoon rose water

1 tablespoon pink clay powder

1 tablespoon triphala powder

½ teaspoon raw honey

a spritz of Citrus-Rose Hydrosol (see page 100)

*Makes enough for 1–2 uses*

Cleanse and dry your skin. Mix all the ingredients (except the Citrus-Rose Hydrosol) together in a small bowl until smooth. Apply the mask to your face with your fingertips, lightly massaging it into your skin to give yourself a slight exfoliation. Leave the mask on for 15–20 minutes—lie down, walk around, or do whatever you like to do while the mask dries. Rinse off the mask with warm water. Mist your skin with the Citrus-Rose Hydrosol.

Any leftover mask will keep for up to 4 days in an airtight container in the refrigerator. When using the mask for the second time, you may need to add a little extra yogurt to the mixture, one drop at a time, to loosen the mask to a useable consistency.

# glowing goddess face oil

This face oil is suitable for all skin types—it will enhance your skin's radiance and keep it supple. You can use the oil as a daily moisturizer or serum, or simply as a special treat when you're in need of some self-love.

2 tablespoons jojoba oil

1 tablespoon sea buckthorn oil

1 tablespoon carrot seed oil

1 tablespoon tamanu oil

1 teaspoon rose hip oil

20–30 drops hyaluronic acid

2 drops of geranium essential oil

**2 drops of frankincense essential oil**
**2 drops of lavender essential oil**
**2 drops of sandalwood essential oil**
**4-fl-oz (120-ml) glass jar or bottle**

*Makes about 4 fl oz (120 ml)*

Mix all the ingredients together in a small bowl. Using a funnel, transfer the oil to the jar or bottle. Massage your face daily with the oil (see page 27).

Store in a cool, dark place. This oil will keep for up to 6 months.

# citrus-rose hydrosol

A hydrosol is simply a misting moisturizer. It is the perfect soothing pick-me-up for your skin and ideal to use before bed to help you wake up feeling refreshed the next morning.

**1–4 mini rose quartz crystals**

**½ cup (120 ml) alkaline or purified water**

**2 drops of colloidal silver**

**1 teaspoon rose water**

**4 drops of citrus essential oil**

**6-fl-oz (175-ml) spray bottle**

*Makes about 4 fl oz (125 ml)*

Place the rose quartz crystals at the bottom of the bottle, then add the remaining ingredients. Shake to mix and it's ready to spray!

This hydrosol should keep for up to 1 month, or even longer if you store it in the refrigerator.

Beauty begins
the moment you decide
to be yourself.

Coco Chanel

# start with self-love

There is an old saying, "If you can't love yourself, how the heck can you love somebody else?" This admittedly cheeky statement actually holds a lot of truth but the bottom line is everything starts with self-love—your health, your self-esteem, your relationships, your success, and your happiness. Even if you had a less than ideal childhood, it is never too late to esteem yourself and watch as everything takes a turn for the better, and quickly.

You can weave this strand of personal empowerment into your life and make sure it grows sure and strong. Your body will recognize when you begin regarding it and treating it like a temple instead of just a vehicle to get from point A to point B. Imprint the positive on body and soul with a simple daily ritual of rubbing on a handmade salve or balm of your choice (see opposite and pages 104–105) after your shower or bath.

By incorporating this ritual into your morning routine, not only will it refresh your spirit every day but, as a bonus, your skin will actually become smoother and softer than silk.

# Sanctifying Salve

Why pay so much for tiny jars full of chemicals when you can whip up a yummy blend of healing herbs and restorative essential oils yourself? It's far cheaper, healthier, and imbued with your personal energy.

1 tablespoon hardened beeswax

5 tablespoons organic oil (sunflower oil is effective and affordable; apricot, jojoba, and avocado oils are nice but quite expensive)

20 drops calendula tincture

10 drops chamomile oil

5 drops lavender oil

½ teaspoon of pure aloe-vera gel

double boiler

whisk and thermometer

small, clean jars with lids

*Makes about 3½ fl oz (100 ml)*

Melt the beeswax with the organic oil in a double boiler (or in a bowl over a saucepan). When the beeswax is fully melted, remove the bowl or pan from the heat. Whisk the mixture until it is cooled to around 100°F (38°C), then stir in the tincture and essential oils along with the aloe vera. Stir gently, thinking of your intended outcome of health, glowing skin, and joy-filled times. The mixture will thicken into a smooth salve but before it stiffens too much, spoon it into the storage jars.

These homemade creams last longer if you keep them refrigerated.

# calming balms

This concoction will not only soothe and nourish the skin, but it is also very good for your soul. The fresh and lightly citrus scent of neroli in combination with vanilla is extremely comforting and tremendously relaxing. The result is so pleasing, you may even consider using it as a perfume.

**1 cup (225 g) shea butter**
**½ cup (125 ml) coconut oil**
**½ cup (125 ml) almond oil**
**15 drops neroli essential oil**
**15 drops vanilla essential oil**
**double boiler**
**wooden spoon and whisk**
**4 x 4-fl oz (125-ml) clean jars with glass lids**

*Makes about 17 fl oz (500 ml)*

Melt the shea butter with the coconut oil in the top of a double boiler. Remove from the heat and allow to cool for 30 minutes. Add in the almond oil (you can substitute olive oil, jojoba oil, or any liquid organic oil) and blend.

When the mixture starts to solidify partially, add in the essential oils. Stir in, and then whip the mixture to a butter-like consistency, which will take only a few minutes. It can be used immediately.

Store the balm in the storage jars in a cool, dry cupboard.

## more mood-boosting balm blends

Try these combinations of essential oils in place of the neroli and vanilla in your calm balm and you will soon discover bliss in a bottle:

- **Mellow Me:** equal parts of chamomile and rose is a gentle, mellowing combination.

- **In Your Groove:** bergamot and basil will help you to get your groove back.

- **Chill Out:** clary sage and ylang ylang pair up nicely to bring you peace of mind.

- **Unwind Your Mind:** jasmine and valerian will sweeten up your mood in a jiffy.

- **Happy Hippie:** lavender and patchouli are a power duo for a quiet mind and upbeat thinking.

- **Sweet Serenity:** lemon balm and vetiver combine for real soothing and letting go.

## blessings rite

Whenever you make your own beauty products,
whether for your own use or as a gift, stop
and count your health blessings with this
mindfulness practice.

Sit in a comfortable position with your newly filled
bottle or jar in a bowl or dish in front of you. Think
about the blessings in your life and the gifts your
particular item offers. Visualize your skin gleaming
with vitality, for example, or picture your loved ones
wearing a big smile as they use your handmade
remedies. What are you grateful for at this
moment? There is a powerful magic in recognizing
all that you possess and in cultivating an attitude of
gratitude. Breathe steadily and deeply, inhaling and
exhaling slowly, for 20 minutes. As you meditate,
visualize sending positive energy into the bowl.
Now the blessings will be there any time you or
a loved one may need them.

a grateful heart is a
magnet for miracles

chapter 4

CARING for YOUR SOUL

# the power of mantras

A mantra is a sacred word, sound, sentence, or phrase that is repeated aloud or sung frequently to enhance vibration and heal the mind-body-spirit. Yogis, gurus, and similar practitioners have used mantras for centuries in the practice of meditation and transformation. Although mantras are mentioned in sacred texts throughout history, we can take a more modern approach to the use of mantras. Anything you want to overcome, transform, change, manifest, or instill in your life can be done through the practice of singing or speaking a mantra aloud.

Mantras are also a wonderful way to connect with a partner or friend. Sitting in a circle or across from one another while singing a mantra can raise the vibrational energy even more. If you would like to explore the work of using mantras more deeply, there are traditional mantras that can be sung along with music.

## speaking your truth

When we hide or dim our inner light from others we suffer. It's important to always speak your truth and use your voice to communicate what's inside of you. What is your truth? It is the essence of you that not only makes you unique but also drives you forward on your journey. Your truth doesn't have to be your job or your career, rather it's a purposeful path that you are on, and when you stray from it you feel an innate pull back toward it.

A mantra can be any saying, phrase, song, etc. that resonates with you. Exercising your voice to say what you want can have a positive effect on the way you communicate outside of your self-care practice. The more you get used to channeling your feelings into words with clarity, the more you will begin to navigate the process of speaking your truth and communicating that truth to others.

# how to perform a mantra

## 1

Find a quiet space and sit comfortably, cross-legged on the floor or with your legs out in front of you. Become mindful of your breath, your body, and how you feel. Sit up tall and activate all the energy flowing through your body. Imagine a string tugging at the top of your head and pulling your spine upright.

## 2

Take a few deep breaths through your nose and into your belly, exhaling through your nose. Place your hands on your heart.

## 3

Once you have tuned into your body, mind, and spirit, begin to repeat your chosen mantra. You can either say the mantra or sing it aloud, exercising your throat chakra. Repeat the mantra aloud for at least five minutes or until you are filled with a sense of joy and the words of the mantra sing throughout your being.

## 4

Close out this sacred practice with a prayer or blessing that you would like to be reminded of throughout the day.

Try the following mantras to raise your vibration, help you cultivate clarity and confidence, and protect your energy.

### self-love mantra:

I am confident, I am radiant, I am filled with joy.

### truth mantra:

I embody my truth.

### protection mantra:

I am safe, I am surrounded by light, my energy is protected.

Three things
cannot be long hidden:
the sun, the moon,
and the truth.

Buddha

# metta mantra meditation

When you've had a rough day at work, your inner critic is overactive, or you are just feeling a little down, try this loving-kindness (*metta*) meditation. It can be difficult to cultivate self-love, but it is one of the most important things you can do for yourself. The very peacefulness you create with this ritual can also be sent to another person.

Begin by sitting quietly, taking relaxed, slow, deep breaths and wishing yourself happiness. After sitting quietly, begin to speak this mantra aloud:

May I be happy, may I be well, may I be safe.

May I be peaceful, may I be at ease.

May I be content.

Continue this practice until you feel full of self-love and compassion. When you are ready to move to the next phase, begin to think of another person to whom you would like to give happiness and unconditional love. Send the love through your meditation and saying these words:

May you be happy, may you be well, may you be safe.

May you be peaceful, may you be at ease.

May you be filled with contentment.

# positive affirmations

Positive thinking may not solve all your problems, but negative thinking can greatly affect your outlook and reaction to life. The more you speak to yourself with negativity, the more you will suffer. Being negative is setting yourself up for failure, whereas being positive gives you an alternative route to finding happiness and peace. If you think positively, you will radiate and spread that upward energy to all areas of your life. Have you ever met someone who exudes happy energy and whose happiness just pours from their being effortlessly? If you have, that person most likely practices (on some level) shifting their energy to be more positive.

The way we think and talk to ourselves also directly affects our health. We always have a choice in life, to succumb to our woes or find new ways to overcome them. If you choose the latter, you will see the difference in your health and overall happiness. However, it is important to find time to revel in your thoughts and emotions and to acknowledge your feelings and not suppress them. When we hold in our emotions, we dull our vibration and manifest dis-ease.

Affirmations are statements or phrases that we repeat regularly to set our intention and bring about change. They can help us stay focused on our goals. If you repeat an affirmation on a daily basis, you are engraining the essence of those words inside your subconscious mind, which will help you remain positive in times of distress.

### morning affirmation

Tape your affirmation to your bathroom mirror and repeat it over and over again while you're doing your morning routine until you're finished.

## compose your own affirmations

As you will discover, when you write your own affirmations, a few of them will "stick" and really hit the spot. Gather some paper cut into squares, your favorite pen, and a votive candle.

### 1

Go to your favorite spot for writing and lay out the paper, pen, and candle. As you light the candle, speak aloud:

*I am strong beyond measure.*

*I am loved beyond measure.*

*I deserve a life of joy and pleasure.*

## 2

Breathe in and out deeply three times and sit down to pen your affirmations. Write at least three, and keep them somewhere you can see them every day, such as your office desk.

Here are some suggestions to start you on your path:

I am a wholly unique person and I celebrate that.

I am open to positive change in my life and welcome it.

Every day, I am healing and growing in wisdom.

You have within
you the strength, the
patience, and the passion
to reach for the stars and
to change the world.

Harriet Tubman

today,
I choose
joy

# touchstones for peace
of mind

A small stack of rocks, known as a cairn, may look purely decorative but it is much more than that. It is an important device to help you be in balance with nature. Many of our modern maladies, such as anxiety, SAD (seasonal affected disorder), tension headaches, depression, and more come about as a result of disconnection from nature. A cairn not only serves as a visual reminder of being in balance, but, when created using healing crystals, its grounding properties are magnified and it will surround you with supporting energies from earth.

Certain crystals can be true touchstones in your life and bring multitudinous benefits, both emotional and spiritual. Find a spot in your home or office where you can incorporate your crystals into each and every day, whether a shrine, your nightstand, or a corner of your desk. This can be your special corner of the world where you can renew and connect with your spiritual center. As well as simply looking at your cairn, picking up and holding your touchstones can be one of the most soul-nourishing small acts of self-care you can do.

# crystal benefits

Different crystals bring different benefits. Select which stones to include in your cairn according to your needs.

---

**Inspiration:** amazonite, aventurine, carnelian, chrysolite, chrysoprase, citrine, green tourmaline, malachite, yellow fluorite

---

**Intuition:** amethyst, azurite, celestite, lapis lazuli, moonstone, selenite, smoky quartz, sodalite, star sapphire, yellow calcite

---

**Love:** amethyst, magnetite, rhodochrosite, rose quartz, twinned rock crystals

---

**Abundance:** bloodstone, carnelian, citrine, dendritic agate, diamond, garnet, hawk's-eye, moss agate, peridot, ruby, tiger's-eye, topaz, yellow sapphire

**Protection:** amber, apache tear, chalcedony, citrine, green calcite, jade, jet, smoky quartz

**Self-belief:** azurite, chalcedony, chrysocolla, green tourmaline, rutilated quartz, tiger's-eye

**Serenity:** amber, aventurine, blue jade, dioptase, Herkimer diamond, jasper, kunzite, moonstone, onyx, peridot, quartz, rhodonite

**Confidence:** carnelian, obsidian, quartz, selenite, sodalite, topaz

**Positive energy:** agate, aventurine, bloodstone, calcite, chalcedony, citrine, dioptase, emerald, garnet, orange calcite, ruby, topaz

**Deep wisdom:** emerald, fluorite, Herkimer diamond, moldavite, serpentine, yellow calcite

# simple home shrine

If something is making you feeling edgy or overwhelmed, there is an easy way to deal with it. Create a shrine at the source of your stress. If the problem is too heavy a workload, use your desk. If it is the onslaught of bad news from cable news, place it near the TV.

## 1

Set up your shrine by placing the following ritual implements on a flat surface in the relevant area:

- A statue of a deity of your choice, a god or goddess who can be your guardian.

- A black crystal, such as obsidian, which absorbs negative energy.

- A white crystal, such as white quartz, which emits positive energy.

- A black votive candle and a white votive candle in glass votive containers; these small votives burn for 3 hours.

- Sage for smudging and a fireproof dish.

- A broom.

- A small bowl containing ½ cup (100 g) of salt.

## 2

Put the black crystal by the black candle and the white one by the white candle. Light both candles and use the black candle to light the sage. Go around the newly designated shrine, room, or area with the sage for a good smudging (energy cleansing—see pages 78–79). Put the sage in the fireproof dish.

## 3

Take up your broom and with light strokes sweep the shrine space thoroughly and brush the negative energy out of the front door.

## 4

Extinguish both the sage and the white candle and place them on your permanent altar. If you don't have one, place them in an area where you will see them regularly, such as on your nightstand. Let the black candle burn down safely in the glass votive container and discard the remains outside your home.

### 5

Get the bowl of salt and place the black crystal in it to cleanse the crystal of unwanted energies. Leave the white crystal by the guardian deity overnight.

### 6

When the new day arrives, thank the deity for protection and leave the statue and the white crystal on your permanent altar, nightstand, or wherever you prefer so you are reminded of protective and positive energy. Take the black crystal out of the salt and leave it on the shrine. Pour the salt onto your front step and sweep it away. Now, savor the serene feeling.

# moon cycles

Have you ever felt intense emotional shifts around the time of a full or new moon? The moon affects human behavior and health through its gravitational pull on bodily fluids, which is why it's important to be aware of the phases of the moon and the things you can do to help balance and clear your energy. Connecting with the moon's cycles will enhance your self-care process and increase your awareness of your physical and emotional body. The moon represents emotions, nurturing, instinctive responses, enlightenment, and the rhythm of time.

## at the full moon

give thanks for your blessings | release anything that is no longer serving you (people, items, emotions) | take a cleansing bath | use Palo Santo smudge sticks to cleanse your ritual space (see page 79) | spend time pampering yourself to recharge | cleanse the energy of any crystals you have under the light of the full moon

You could use bergamot essential oil to accompany you during this moon cycle.

## at the new moon

clean out the cobwebs in your life | let go of negative patterns and habits that no longer serve you | physically clean your house and personal space | meditate | set intentions for this new cycle and focus on all the things you aspire to accomplish (see opposite)

You could use cypress essential oil to accompany you during this moon cycle.

## manifest with the moon

Manifest your dreams by writing them on a clean piece of paper at the time of the new moon. Read them out loud and carry the paper with you throughout the cycle of the moon. When the full moon arrives, burn the paper in a fire, sending the energy up into the universe and trusting it will come into your life.

# living life with a grateful heart

There is much more to gratitude than giving, receiving, and saying thank you. It is a subtly positive way to gradually transform not only your world, but also the world of those around you—and, beyond that, the world we all live in. Gratitude can make great things happen because it has the capacity to open our hearts and show us the art of possibility. Feeling thankful is not always easy, but it offers a pathway to acceptance, in all its forms.

Whole-hearted gratitude is an uplifting, expansive, and positive way of being that leads to appreciation and times of fun and laughter. Sharing, caring, and togetherness are some of the essentials of being human. Feeling thankful makes us want to give back—to those who have helped us, cared for us, who love us—or who quite simply make us happy.

134

a beautiful life
begins with
a beautiful mind

## creating a gratitude altar

Altars have played an important part in rites and rituals of thanksgiving since prehistoric times, as well as being an anchor point for receiving the sacrament in Western religions. They cross cultures and are often mobile, too. Armies use the drum as an altar in the battlefield (and still hold drumhead services to this day), and spiritual leaders around the world carry simple symbols of prayer with them at all times, in case of need.

Just as we may light a candle in remembrance or as a sign of peace, or display objects on a desk or mantelpiece to remind us of important moments in our lives, so an altar provides a surface where we can focus our attention and change our thought processes for a moment.

Creating an altar is very personal. If you feel moved to make one in your home, think about whether you want it to be in a place that is light and bright in the morning, or cozy and softly lit for use in the evenings. Do you want to be able to hear sounds of birdsong outside your window, or do you want silence or music so that you can shut out the world?

## items for your altar

- Candles—scented or unscented

- Flowers

- Natural elements, such as pebbles, shells, and/or leaves

- Symbols that have personal meaning for you, such as a ring, crystals, or a sacred object

Altars provide a focus for offering thanks for all that life provides. Put to one side any doubts and preconceptions you may have about whether this will work, and allow yourself the time to create a beautiful space that makes you want to give from your heart, and open yourself up to greater understanding.

# gratitude blessing

This blessing has been inspired by the Buddhist practitioner and teacher Jack Kornfield. His many books are highly respected and his website is a rich source of ideas for meditation practice. His work consistently explains the rich value that such practice offers us in developing a more open-hearted, joyful, and grateful approach to life.

Sit quietly and relax. Take a deep breath and then let go. Listen to your breath as you breathe in and out quietly and naturally. Allow your body to release all tension and become ready to receive this blessing:

I offer my gratitude to the universe and all that is in it, for:

the friends I have been given;

the family I have been given;

the joy of life that I have been given;

the state of health and well-being that I have been given;

*the neighbors that I have been given;*

*the teachers that I have been given;*

*the wisdom that I have been given;*

*the beauty of this earth, and the animals and birds
that we have all been given;*

*my life and all that I have been given.*

Continue to breathe in and out gently. Picture someone you care
about, and think about them as they go about their daily life—and
about the happiness and success you wish for them. With each breath,
offer them your thanks from the bottom of your heart:

*May you always have joy in your heart.*

*May you always enjoy good fortune.*

*May your happiness continue to increase.*

*May you always have peace and well-being on this earth.*

Be happy for this moment.
This moment is your life.

Omar Khayyam

# credits

## text credits

© **Noelle Renée Kovary:** pages 10–12, 14–24, 26–29, 32–35, 37–41, 48–55, 59–61, 64–66, 72–73, 78–79, 82–84, 86–87, 90–100, 102–106, 110–113, 118–119, 131–133

© **Brenda Knight:** pages 26 (Invigorating essential oils), 35 (Relaxing essential oils), 62–63, 68–71, 80–81, 89, 114–115, 120–121, 125–130

© **Sarah Sutton:** 134, 136–139

## image credits

© **Hannah Davies:** pages 11, 14, 17, 22, 28, 29, 33, 34, 35, 39, 40, 48, 50, 51, 52, 62, 79, 83, 86, 87, 89, 91, 92, 129, 130, 137, 142, 143

© **Shutterstock.com:**

Baleika Tamara: pages 6–7, 32–33, 34–35, 37, 40–41, 44, 66, 68–69, 70–71, 72–73, 90–91, 116–117, 134, 136–137, 138–139 (watercolor dots)

Irina Strelnikova: pages 20, 27, 94, 95, 96, 97, 98, 99

Kirill Mlayshev: pages 60, 61

lalan: pages 10–11, 12, 59, 60–61, 62–63, 125, 126–127 (swirls border)

Margarita Manish: pages 131, 133

Nadiinko: pages 126, 127

Nadya Galanicheva: pages 48, 50–51, 52–53, 54–55, 102, 104, 106, 128, 129, 130 (dashed line border)

nani888: pages 2–3, 8–9, 24, 27, 46–47, 68, 76–77, 83, 87, 108–109, 113, 116, 117, 119, 120, 121, 132, 138, 139 (watercolor wash)

Nicetoseeya: pages 1, 16–17, 19, 20–21, 22–23, 24, 26–27, 28–29, 64–65, 78–79, 82–83, 84, 86–87, 88–89, 110–111, 112–113, 131, 132–133 (ovals border)

oxygen_8: pages 24, 81

Perekotypole: pages 5, 14–15, 80–81, 92–93, 94–95, 96–97, 98–99, 100, 118–119, 120–121 (zigzags)

Rimma Z: pages 2, 9, 30, 31, 42, 43, 47, 56, 57, 74, 75, 77, 101, 109, 114, 115, 122, 123, 140, 141 (wreaths)

Rochelle Connolley: pages 6-7, 15, 19, 38–39

Veleri: pages 13, 18, 25, 36, 45, 49, 58, 67, 85, 88, 107, 124, 135, 144

WarmWorld: page 91 (music notes)

every day

is a new start